Feeling... Angry

First published in 1996
This edition 1999

© Franklin Watts 1996

Franklin Watts
96 Leonard Street
London EC2A 4RH

Franklin Watts Australia
14 Mars Road
Lane Cove
NSW 2006

Series editor: Helen Lanz
Series designer: Kirstie Billingham

A CIP catalogue record for this book
is available from the British Library.

ISBN 0 7496 3564 9

10 9 8 7 6 5 4 3 2 1

Dewey Classification 152.4

Printed at Oriental Press, Dubai, U. A. E.

Feeling... Angry

Sally Hewitt

Illustrated by Rhian Nest James

W
FRANKLIN WATTS
LONDON • NEW YORK • SYDNEY

Maya is seven years old. She lives with her mum and dad and her older brother Nathan. Nathan and Maya usually get on really well, but sometimes Nathan makes Maya angry. When Maya gets angry she feels like spoiling things.

Do you feel angry sometimes?

George is Maya's best friend.
He is six years old.
George lives with his mum and his little sister Polly.
George likes to come and play with Maya,
but sometimes he gets angry.
When he feels angry, he sulks and won't play any more.

What do you do when you feel angry?

George has come to play with Maya. He has been looking forward to playing with her all morning. "Come on, let's play treasure hunts," he says excitedly. "Take Polly in the garden with you," says his mum.

George doesn't want Polly to play with them.
"Oh Mum! Polly's too little to play properly. She'll spoil everything," he says.
But Maya takes Polly's hand and they go outside together.

"What shall we play?" says Maya.
"Puppies!" says Polly.
George feels very cross and sulky. He is disappointed.
He doesn't want his little sister to join in their game.
"I'm not playing a baby's game," he says.

Maya has a great idea.
"We can play treasure hunts <u>and</u> puppies," she says.
"Woof! Woof!" says Polly and pretends to wag her tail.
She makes George laugh. "You look funny, Polly," he says.
He forgets to be angry any more.

Mum comes into the garden. She looks very fierce.
"You're covered in mud!" she says, and thinks about all the extra washing.
"What have you been doing?"
"Hunting for treasure," says George.
"Woof! Woof!" says Polly.

Mum starts to laugh.
"You look very funny," she says.
"Are you still angry?" says George.
"I can't be angry while I'm laughing," says Mum.
"Are you still angry George?"
"Oh no," says George. "I've been too busy to be angry."

They go inside and wash off the mud.
"I'll get my new felt-tip pens and we can do some drawing," says Maya.
She looks for her pens, but she can't find them in her bedroom.

They are in Nathan's bedroom, on the floor, with all the lids off.
Maya is really angry with Nathan.
"Look what you've done to my pens," she shouts.
"You've spoilt them. They'll dry up and be no good at all."
Maya is very upset with Nathan. She wants to take the lids off all his new pens and throw them on the floor.

Dad comes in. "What's all the noise about?" he says.
"Nathan's horrible!" says Maya.
"He's spoiled my pens so now I'm going to spoil his pens, too."

"Nathan shouldn't have done that, Maya," says Dad. "I understand why you're angry, but if you spoil his pens, you won't have any pens to draw with at all."
"Shut your eyes and count to ten and think about something nice," he suggests.

Maya shuts her eyes tightly and thinks so hard about going to George's birthday party that she counts all the way up to thirty.
While Maya's eyes are shut, Nathan quickly picks up the pens and puts the lids back on.

When Maya opens her eyes, Nathan gives her the pens.
"I'm sorry Maya. You can borrow Big Teddy if you like."
Maya gives Big Teddy a hug and doesn't feel angry any more.

"I'm going to draw a dinosaur," says George.
"I'm going to draw a picture of me," says Maya.
George's dinosaur looks very fierce.
Maya's picture doesn't look at all like Maya.

George laughs. "You look just like a dinosaur in your picture," he says.
"I don't!" says Maya.

She is furious because she thinks George's picture is much better than hers and now he is teasing her about it. She hates her picture and she wants to tear it up.
"It's a stupid picture," she shouts.

"Why is it a stupid picture?" asks Mum.
"It doesn't look like me, it looks like a dinosaur," shouts Maya.
Mum gives Maya her mirror.
"You do look a <u>bit</u> like a fierce dinosaur, Maya," says Mum.
She gives Maya a big smile to cheer her up.

Maya tries hard not to smile, but she can't help it.
"That's better," says Mum. "Look at yourself in the mirror now and draw what you see."
"That's a good picture of you, Maya," says George. "You don't look like a fierce dinosaur at all."

Maya's mum pins their pictures up on the wall.
"Let's play Snap," says Maya. She is very good at Snap.
"You always win Snap," grumbles George.
"I know," says Maya.

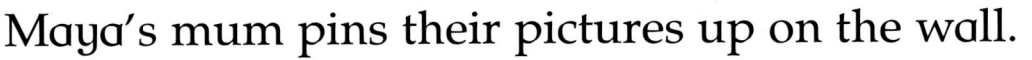

They play three games of Snap and Maya wins all the games!
George feels very angry with her. He hates losing games.
Everyone likes to win sometimes.
"It's not fair!" he says. "You're not my friend any more."

George sits under the table and sulks while Maya and Polly help to make some buns. He soon gets very bored and the buns smell delicious.
"You're missing all the fun, George," says his mum.

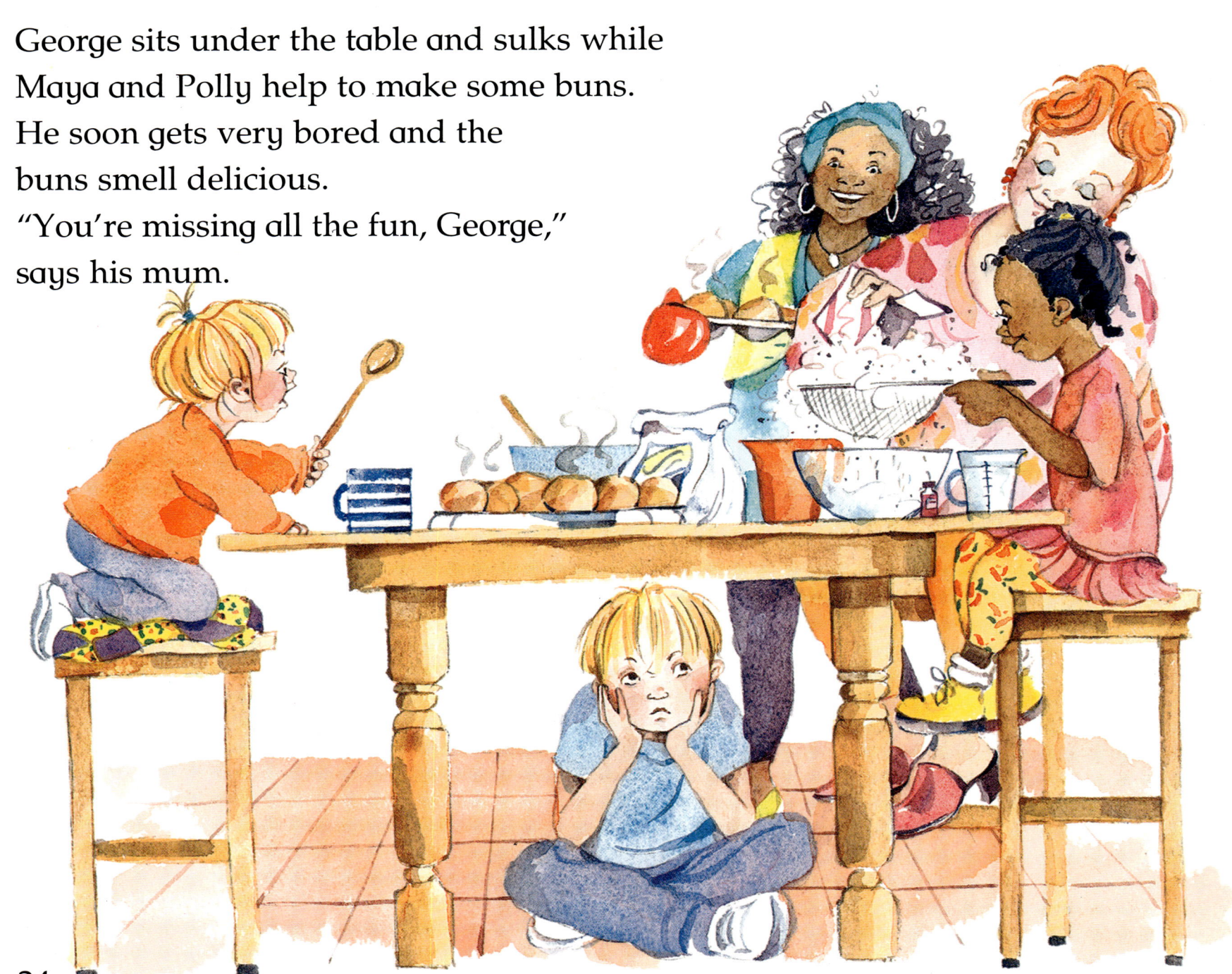

George comes out from under the table.
"What can I do?" he asks.
Maya is glad that George is joining in again.
She gives him the icing to spread on the buns.
He doesn't feel bored or angry any more.

On the way home, Polly sees a little girl with a red balloon.
"Balloon!" shouts Polly holding out her hand.
"No," says Mum. "It's not for you."
Polly screams and shouts. She is too little to understand that she can't have everything she wants all the time.

George feels embarrassed. He wants Polly to stop crying.
"Oh, look Polly!" says George. "A big yellow digger is digging a hole in the road."
Polly stops screaming and watches the digger.

"Well done, George," whispers Mum.
"The digger made Polly forget to be angry."
"Maya got angry twice today," says George.
"So did you," says Mum.
"Being angry spoils everything," says George.

"I wasn't angry when I was busy and Maya stopped being angry when she thought about my birthday party," says George. "Sometimes I take big breaths and count to ten to stop me feeling angry," says Mum. "Sometimes I shout at my Teddy," says George.

What do you do to stop feeling angry?

Notes for teachers and parents

Children's feelings of anger can lead to frustration, disappointment, tears and tantrums. By their very nature, feelings can be difficult to understand and discuss, for adults as well as children.

Sometimes feeling angry can be justifiable, sometimes it can be completely inappropriate, but it's important to understand what has generated the feeling and to learn how to cope with it. Through trying to understand emotions, strategies can be learned about how to deal with them, and what can be done about the situation that caused them in the first place.

In the story, George and Maya are confronted with situations that make them angry. These incidents can be used as starting points to discuss what can make children feel angry; they may recognise some of their own behaviour in the story or be able to understand why someone has behaved in a certain way towards them.

The adults in the story provide helpful support for the children. They are used as a way to highlight the reasons behind the anger in each situation, or to offer solutions, providing an insight that children themselves might not be aware of.

The following questions about some of the incidents in the story could be used to generate some discussion.

Further discussion and activities

- On page 8, George feels very cross and sulky because his mum has made him play with his little sister in the garden.

What does "cross" mean? Do you or your friend have a little brother or sister? Have they ever made you cross? What did they do to make you cross?

- George stops being angry on page 9. What cheers him up? What cheers you up and helps you to stop feeling angry?

- Maya is really angry with Nathan on page 13. What did Nathan do? How does Nathan help Maya to stop feeling angry?

- When George and Maya play Snap on page 23, George says he doesn't want to be Maya's friend any more. Why doesn't he want to be her friend?

- Do your friends sometimes make you angry? What sort of thing makes you feel angry with them?

- Have you ever made a friend angry? What did you do? Can you think of a way to stop your friend from feeling angry with you?

- If you are angry, or if someone is angry with you, it can help to talk to someone you love and trust about how you feel.

It might be helpful to follow up the discussion or story with some activities. Some suggested activities are listed below:

- Make a list of ideas in the story that can help you stop feeling angry. Which is your favourite idea? You could try it the next time you feel angry.

- George and Polly have been making play-dough models. They have made an awful mess! George is angry because Mum has put Polly to bed and he has to clear up the mess on his own.

Draw a picture or write a story about what happens next to stop George feeling angry.

Useful words

angry — A feeling you get when something really annoys you. You can feel angry for a lot of different reasons.

bored — If you have nothing to do, or you have to do the same thing over and over again, it can make you feel bored.

cross — This is another word for angry or being in a bad mood.

disappointed — A feeling you can get when something doesn't turn out as well as you wanted it to or when you feel let down.

embarrassed — A feeling you can get if everyone notices you when you don't want them to, or if you or someone else has done something which has made you feel silly.

fierce — Someone is fierce if they are rough or bullying, or if they behave in a way that frightens you. People sometimes behave in a fierce way if they are angry or cross.

glad — Feeling glad is when you feel pleased or happy about something.

grumble — This is when you complain or moan about something that you don't like or that has made you unhappy.

to spoil something — This is when someone purposely ruins something that someone else is doing. For example, if you are drawing a picture and someone scribbles on it, that person has spoilt your picture.

sulk — This is when you feel bad tempered or upset and so you might go off on your own. Often if you are sulking, you go quiet and think to yourself, "it isn't fair!".